D0940111

HOW TO RAISE A
GREAT
STUDENT

HOW TO RAISE A
GREAT
STUDENT

The Ultimate Guide to
Raising the Best Student
YOU Possibly Can

THOMAS ROBERTS

© 2007 Thomas Roberts

How to Raise a Great Student:
The Ultimate Guide to Raising the Best Student YOU Possibly Can

All rights reserved. No part of this book may be used or reproduced in any manner whatsoever without permission.

Empower YOUniversity™ books may be purchased for educational, business, or sale promotional use. For information, please write Program and Projects Department, Empower YOUniversity, Post Office Box 3368, Merrifield, VA 22116.

Empower YOUniversity™ is a division of Roberts Education Corp™ and a member of the Great Student Network™.

Roberts Education Corp™, Empower YOUniversity™, and Great Student Network™ are trademarks of Roberts Education Corp.

First Edition

ISBN–13: 978-1-934616-68-0
ISBN–10: 1-934616-68-0

Empower YOUniversity

*"Providing YOU the Fundamentals
to Win in the Game of Life"*

AUTHOR'S NOTE TO YOU

Congratulations on taking another positive step in raising your child. YOU have the ability to help your child become all that he/she can be, but it will take a committed effort, patience, and tons of unconditional love.

YOU are the best influence, role model, and source of inspiration that your child could ever have. Treat that responsibility respectfully and take the challenge to be a positive, encouraging, and fully present participant in your child's life.

Children that perform best at school typically have engaged and involved parents or caregivers who understand who their children are, what their children are capable of, and work diligently to provide their children with the proper training, tools, and boundaries to help them be successful.

This book will provide YOU with the training and tools that YOU will need to connect with your child in order to help him/her become the absolute best student he/she can be. However, the most important ingredients to raising a great student are solely up to YOU: unconditional love, positive reinforcement and affirmation, and consistent support and participation in your child's life.

Let's get started.

Thomas Roberts

HOW TO USE RAGS

How to Raise a Great Student is not just a book. It is a parent's or caregiver's:

- Personal tutor.

- Positive and helpful parental companion.

- Detailed road map for helping your child achieve success in school.

- Comprehensive resource and training guide for interacting with your child.

- Comprehensive resource and training guide for participating in your child's educational experience.

- Inspirational and motivational tool.

How to Raise a Great Student is an action-based text that is designed to help YOU become an *active* supporter of your child's educational goals. It is written in a clear, simple, and easy to understand format, use of language, and structure. Each parent point is presented on its own page and then immediately explained and reinforced on the adjacent page in order to help YOU see the message, grasp and understand it quickly, and then explain "how to use" what YOU just learned and "why" that lesson is important for YOU to know and understand. The chapters are structured specifically to help YOU prepare for your child's educational experiences.

How to Raise a Great Student was not written to be read once or memorized, then left on the shelf. It should be constantly reviewed, read, and considered. This book is a dynamic and interactive tool. To get the best results, YOU should:

- Skim the entire text before YOU concentrate on one particular parent point.

- Concentrate on one parent point at a time and a maximum of three per day.

- Digest and utilize the material in small bits.

- Focus on the parent point that YOU find most helpful and impacting first.

- Read a parent point, practice it, and work to implement it into your parenting style.

- Practice the parent point YOU desire to learn repeatedly until YOU get it right and it becomes a positive parental habit or behavior for YOU.

- Commit yourself to getting better.

- Maintain a positive, determined, and driven attitude throughout the process.

- Do not get deterred or distraught over mistakes.

- Be patient with yourself. Some of the parent points are easier to implement than others.

- Buy *How to Be a Great Student* for yourself and your child to teach your child the educational fundamentals required to become a great student.

If YOU learn, try, practice, develop, and implement the great parenting habits and behaviors in this book, YOU will significantly improve your relationship with your child, become a positive and active presence in your child's educational experience, and take control of your child's educational experience.

The best thing about this book is that it can always be with YOU. Keep it nearby. Whenever YOU need a refresher or reminder, pull it out, review the appropriate parent point, and get back on track.

TABLE OF CONTENTS

CHAPTER ONE

Turn Your Home into a Learning Environment

Create an environment for learning in your home

How?

- Establish a "learning zone" in your home.
  - ○ This should be a location in your home where reading, studying, and working is encouraged and protected.
- Create a work, read, and study area in your home.
  - ○ The kitchen table is a great location.
- Make activities, reading, learning, and doing new things a part of your home.

Parent Point #2

Make learning fun!

- Make learning and the pursuit of education fun.
- Teach your child to enjoy the learning process.
- Encourage and support your child.
  - Learn the difference between pressure and encouragement.
- Celebrate your child's school accomplishments and achievements (big or small).
- Refer to learning and education with a smile and positive comments.

Establish an educational culture and routine in your home

Quality preparation, learning, and being responsible are habits.

- Create a routine for dinner, study time, family time, and bedtime.

- Create a mandatory study or review time during the week.

- Lead the way. The best influence is your example through your actions.

- Learn new things yourself.

- Celebrate learning and accomplishing new things routinely in your home.

Create an interactive home where parent–child dialogue is encouraged, expected, and required

- Interact with your child daily.
- Ask open-ended questions about school.
  - How was your day?
  - What did YOU learn, do, and try?
  - Who did YOU talk to, play with, have lunch with, etc.?
- Ask a question and then listen intently to your child's response.
  - Listen carefully to his/her response.
  - Pay attention to how he/she replies to your questions.
  - Learn and remember who and what your child talks about.
- Regularly obtain verbal downloads regarding your child's day.
- Create conversations, not lectures.

Parent Point #5

Respect when your child is doing his/her schoolwork

Help your child learn by:

- Being quiet.

- Reading words/terms to your child.

- Being available to help your child when he/she has questions.

- Not interrupting your child's study time.

Parent Point #6

Make your house a "home"

Children need love, structure, and support to do well outside of the house and that comes from what they develop and feel inside of your home.

- Make your home a loving, supportive, positive, and peaceful place.

- Establish an environment based on mutual respect, positive interactions, and supporting and affirming communication.

- Make your home a place where your child is "comfortable."

- Make sure your child always feels welcome and loved at home.

- Make sure your child feels home is a safe place.

- Make sure there are rules, structure, and expectations of how your child behaves at home as well as in public.

Parent Point #7

If your home is a challenging environment, recommend that your child leave "home" at home

Suggest to your child:

- Do whatever YOU can to leave "home" at home.

- Focus on learning at school.

- Spend time at school, do your very best, and get involved in as many positive activities as YOU can handle without negatively impacting your grades.

- Talk with an adult YOU trust about your situation.

- Get help and advice from counselors.

CHAPTER TWO

Know and Understand Your Child

Understand your child

- To truly help your child, YOU must develop a realistic appraisal and understanding of:

  ○ Who your child is

  ○ What he/she is good at

  ○ Areas where he/she needs improvement

  ○ What his/her interests and natural talents are

- Your child's educational success depends on your ability to ensure that your child is being taught in ways that are most appropriate for his/her skill level, learning ability, and passions and natural gifts (see Parent Point #9).

Determine how your child learns best

How does your child remember things best?

What works best for your child?

Here are the different ways that children learn:

- Auditory or by hearing
  - Does your child remember things better when he/she hears them or when someone tells them to him/her?
- Visual or by seeing
  - Does your child remember things better when he/she sees or reads them?
- Kinesthetic or by doing
  - Does your child remember things better by "doing" or learning through action?

Determine the best learning environment that suits your child's talents, skills, and needs

Every child is different.

The proper learning environment materially improves a student's learning experience and ability to perform.

- Whenever possible, enroll your child in a school that fits his/her gifts, talents, and needs.

- Do all that YOU can to find the best "fit" for your child's abilities, personality, and skill level.

- Consider your child's learning style (how he/she best learns—see Parent Point #9):

  - Auditory or hearing—learning by hearing

  - Visual or seeing—learning by reading or seeing

  - Kinesthetic or doing—learning by action or doing

- Then, look for learning environments that match up with your child's learning style.

  - For example, a child who learns better by doing (kinesthetic) will do better in a class that places greater emphasis on hands-on learning activities.

Parent Point #11

Get to know your child

- What does your child enjoy?
- What is your child good at?
- What is hard for your child?
- What is easy for your child?
- What would your child like to be?
- What truly captivates your child?
- What does your child love to do?

Be able to "read" your child

- Learn your child's various signals and patterns of behavior. They will tell YOU when your child is:
  - Happy
  - Sad
  - Angry
  - Scared
  - Confused
  - Frustrated
  - Hurt
  - Uncomfortable
  - Distressed
  - In need of your help
- Always be aware of how your child is responding.
  - Ask open-ended questions to get your child to speak more freely.
- Respond with affection and attention when YOU see that something is "off" with your child.

Parent Point #13

Realistically assess what your child is capable of

Having a realistic understanding of your child's abilities removes pressure on all involved because it keeps both YOU and your child from having "unfair expectations."

- What is your child able to do?

- What does his/her best effort look like?

- When your child does his/her absolute best, what have been the results?

- How do YOU know when your child has given his/her all?

Communicate with your child every day

- Ask questions.
- Listen to learn about your child.
- Pay attention to what your child is and is not saying.
- Encourage your child.
- Learn his/her fears, goals, and motivations.
- Acknowledge, praise, and reward the behaviors and choices that YOU desire.

CHAPTER THREE

Avoid the "Perfection Trap"

Avoid the horrible "perfection trap"

Instead of expecting perfection, expect your child's very best effort.

The relentless pursuit of perfection:

- Is impossible to sustain.

- Is rarely attainable every time.

- Destroys self-confidence.

- Creates a feeling of insecurity and inferiority because your child begins to believe that YOU will only love him/her when he/she does not make mistakes.

- Interferes and, typically, blocks a healthy and open parent–child relationship.

Handle bad or troubling news, disappointment, and poor decisions and behavior with poise and control

- No matter what YOU believe, your child will make mistakes.

- Loyalty and commitment are earned in times of crisis, failure, and disappointment.

- YOU must show your child that YOU will be there for him/her—in good times and bad.

- YOU can admonish and punish your child's actions/behaviors while loving, nurturing, and supporting your child.

- YOU can correct your child's decision-making process or negative actions without destroying your child's confidence or self-worth.

Seek your child's best effort, not PERFECTION!

- Your child's best effort—not perfection—should be the target.

  ○ Encourage, ask for, and expect your child's best effort.

  ○ To be fair to your child, have realistic expectations for what his/her best truly is.

  ○ Nurture, support, and reward your child's best effort even if the results fall short.

- YOU want to develop and instill respect of commitment, focus, and effort.

- YOU never want your children to think that YOU will only love them, if/when they are perfect.

---

*Critique and correct
your child's inappropriate
actions and behaviors,
not the child*

Correct the actions, not the child

- Pinpoint the item, action, or behavior that YOU want to correct.

- Separate your child's actions from your child.

- Correct the behavior, decision-making process, and/or the bad actions taken.

- Focus on the decisions that led to the poor choice or unacceptable result.

- Include your child in the "appropriate decisions/behaviors" solution discussion.

- Clearly communicate what YOU expect from your child going forward.

- At the end of the conversation, hug your child with love.

Parent Point #19

*Teach your child
that mistakes are nothing
to fear*

Mistakes are nothing to fear. In fact, they are a vital part of the learning process.

Remind your child:

- When YOU do not know how to do something, do not expect to always get it correct the first time.

- If YOU are afraid to make a mistake, YOU will rarely learn anything new.

- Mistakes do not mean that YOU are dumb. They simply mean that YOU ARE LEARNING!

CHAPTER FOUR

Be an
Active Parent

Parent Point #20

Attend school and extracurricular activities

Nothing says and shows YOU care and believe in your child more than being present and involved.

- When YOU attend school or extracurricular activities, focus on the event, not talking.

- Smile, relax, and enjoy the event.

- After the event, tell your child how proud YOU are of him/her—and mean it.

- Ask your child questions about the performance:

  ○ How did he/she think it went?

  ○ What was his/her favorite part?

  ○ How did it feel to . . . ?

- Tell your child what YOU enjoyed about the performance.

- Positively affirm your child. Regardless of how big or small the action is, point out something that your child did well.

- Greet your child with a big smile and a hug after the performance—good or bad. This says, "I love YOU and I am here for YOU"—always.

Parent Point #21

Attend all parent–teacher conferences

- Be prepared to discuss your child's performance and behavior at school.

- Have knowledge and records of your child's grades, assignment scores, and work history before the meeting.

- Be open.

- Ask questions about your child's demeanor, participation, and comfort in class.

- Ask for specific feedback regarding your child's performance.

- Ask the teacher to describe his/her educational style.

- Develop a rapport and relationship with your child's educators.

Know your parental and child's rights in the school system

Review the rules, regulations, and by-laws of your child's school and the school system.

- Learn:
  - ○ The specific requirements for advancing or graduating.
  - ○ Exactly where your child stands in relation to what is required to advance or graduate.
  - ○ What resources are available to YOU and your child.
  - ○ Who the leaders of your child's school and school system are.
  - ○ What programs and assistance are available.
  - ○ The procedures for corrective action.
- Visit your school or school system's website.
- Request all available literature for parents or caregivers from the school's guidance counselor.
- Review all school mailings, calendars, and brochures.

Introduce yourself to your child's educators

YOU will have better results when your child's educators know that YOU are an active participant in his/her education.

Good educators want your presence, assistance, and participation.

- Be present at your child's school. It will have a positive impact.

- Develop a rapport with your child's educators.

- Provide your child's educators easy access to YOU (phone numbers and, if applicable, an e-mail address).

- Make sure everyone—your child and his/her educators—understands through your words and deeds that YOU will be a full participant in your child's education.

- Make sure that your child's educators understand that YOU expect to be informed of your child's progress, performance, and participation at school.

Join the Parent Teacher Association (PTA)

It's a great way to:

- Participate in your child's school experience.
- Learn more about your child's school.
- Familiarize yourself with school protocol, regulations, curriculum, and events.
- Demonstrate your commitment to your child's education.
- Learn about the culture at your child's school.
- Interact with your child's educators.
- Meet other parents.

Read and review all school literature

- Read and review:
  - ○ Newsletters
  - ○ Calendars
  - ○ Letters from the principal/head of school
  - ○ Websites—both the school's and the school system's
- Coordinate your family calendar around important school functions and events.
- Stay informed.
- Track and plan for events, tests, etc.
- Show your child that YOU value him/her, that his/her education is a priority, and that YOU are paying attention.
- Look for important information on:
  - ○ What is taking place at school
  - ○ Who is participating and required to attend
  - ○ When it is
  - ○ Where it will be

Keep a school calendar at home and use it

- Show your child that education is important by displaying the school calendar prominently. This is a subtle yet positive statement and affirmation for your child.

- Organize your family calendar accordingly.

- Always account for your child's outings, events, and test dates when making family plans.

- Know and remember when test dates are and assignments are due—and follow up with your child. Ask your child:

  ○ How do YOU feel the test or assignment went?

  ○ What was your score or grade?

  ○ What did YOU get correct?

  ○ What mistakes did YOU make? What caused the mistake? How can YOU correct it?

  ○ What did YOU learn?

- Discuss school openly, calmly, and positively.

- Always end with a positive affirmation of your child, a smile, and a hug, then move forward.

Participate and help at your child's school

- Be present and involved at your child's school.

- Participate in activities that interest YOU.

- Lead volunteer activities at school where YOU have a particular skill or gift.

- Periodically chaperone functions.

- Volunteer whenever YOU can.

  ○ This is a great way to observe every aspect of your child's learning environment.

  ○ It reinforces to your child that YOU are invested in his/her educational experience.

  ○ It provides YOU a chance to evaluate your child's learning environment without the filter or slant of anyone else.

  ○ It validates your child because your mere presence communicates that YOU care about your child.

Respect your child's educators; do not fear them

- Challenge your child's educators maturely when YOU sense a problem, mistake, or misconduct.

- Do not be afraid to question administrators or educators. Educators are human, and, therefore, they are capable of making mistakes, too.

- Look for facts and actions, not opinions or emotions.

- Ask detailed questions and require educators to thoroughly address your concerns.

- Use facts and actual records to support your position regarding your child.

- Remain calm, composed, and poised throughout your interactions and exchanges with your child's educators.

Conduct yourself with dignity and class at all times, but especially at school

Your child learns how to handle stress, disappointments, and frustration from observing how YOU handle them.

- Remember to be the example for your child.

- Keep your composure.

- Keep your emotions under control.

- Treat others with the respect that YOU expect and deserve.

- Handle all conflict and disagreements maturely.

Never show up an educator, even when he/she is wrong

- Praise in public; chastise in private.

- Even when YOU have to challenge or criticize an educator or school administrator, do so respectfully and privately.

  ○ Establish an appointment to discuss the matter one-on-one.

  ○ If others are around, pull the educator aside, then calmly and respectfully express your concern.

During moments of conflict and tension at school, focus on the facts, truths, and actions of all involved, not emotions, perceptions, or hearsay

During moments of conflict and tension at school, do not get caught up in emotions, perceptions, or hearsay.

- Focus on the problem, not the person.

- Remain focused on why YOU are there.

- Remain calm. Anger and attacks only create wedges, not solutions.

- Gather and expect facts.

- Fully understand the problem or conflict before YOU explore solutions.

- Ask the educator or administrator:

  ○ What would YOU recommend?

  ○ What can we do now?

  ○ What should we do now?

  ○ What do YOU consider to be the best solution?

CHAPTER FIVE

Learn What YOU Can Do

Set a positive tone toward learning and education in your home

- Embrace education and learning in your home.
- Support learning early in your child's life.
- Create an expectation and passion for learning.
- Positively reinforce and acknowledge learning at home.

Parent Point #33

Be a positive influence

- Set the bar high.

- Believe in your child.

- Invest in your child.

- Be present mentally, physically, and emotionally.

- Provide positive reinforcement when your child does well.

- Nurture and support your child even when he/she makes mistakes or does not perform well.

- Affirm your child's efforts—even when he/she does not perform well—with a smile, hug, and a sincere "I love YOU."

- Always remind your child that YOU believe in him/her.

- Tell your child that YOU are proud of him/her regularly!

  ○ Reinforce that statement through positive, supportive, and encouraging actions.

Make sure YOU and your child read How to Be a Great Student

- It will provide YOU with fundamental lessons, training, and tools to help YOU teach your child what it takes to become a great student.

- Parents or caregivers who take the time to teach their children typically have the greatest impact on a child's success throughout his/her life.

- The book will help reinforce the behaviors and actions that YOU expect from your child.

  ○ Make these points a part of your lessons and teachings.

- *How to Be a Great Student* is your child's:

  ○ Positive school companion

  ○ Constant reminder of to how to behave

  ○ Detailed guide for success at school

  ○ Personal tutor

  ○ Tailored support system

  ○ Gift from YOU and positive reminder of your support

Discuss How to Be a Great Student *with your child in supportive one-on-one sessions at home*

The lessons in *How to Be a Great Student* will empower your child through increased confidence, enhanced skills, and your participation. Take the time to discuss this guide with your child in one-on-one sessions at home.

Why?

- Offers a proven way to educate your child.

- Shows your child that YOU believe in him/her and are committed to his/her education.

- Shows your child that he/she is not alone.

- Builds trust between YOU and your child.

- Gives YOU more credibility because the lessons are from an "outside authority."

- Provides a great opportunity to communicate and share.

- Helps your children understand their responsibility and accountability for their performance, which directly impacts their future, education, and success.

Teach your child a good learning attitude

Remind your child that:

- The better your attitude and effort are toward learning, the more help YOU will receive, the more YOU will learn, and the more YOU will get out of your education.

- Negative energy blocks your ability to think, concentrate, and absorb knowledge.

- YOU will learn more when YOU take a positive approach versus a fearful or defeated attitude.

Help your child own his/her success

- Hold your child accountable for his/her actions and behavior.

- If YOU decide certain behaviors will be punished, follow through with the appropriate punishment.

- Be consistent in how YOU react.

- Establish goals, targets, and expectations with your child. Involve him/her in the process.

- Teach your child that he/she is ultimately responsible for how his/her life turns out.

- Encourage your child to make great decisions.

  ○ Use real-life examples and situations that occur around YOU as opportunities to discuss and evaluate the good or bad choices of others.

  ○ Discuss and explore situations before they happen to your child.

  ○ Explain to your child what good choices are, how they are made, and the self-respecting thought process that is required to make smart choices.

---

*Remember that success
is up to your child*

- There is a saying: "YOU can lead a horse to water, but YOU cannot make it drink." That is especially true with children.

- As a parent, YOU can show your child the right path, but it is up to him/her to walk it.

- Positive reinforcement and parent participation have tremendous influence on children.

  ○ Do what YOU can to teach, instill, and develop good preparation, study, and learning habits.

- The four components of learning are training, tools, time, and effort. Tell your child:

  ○ With the proper training, tools, time, and effort, YOU can learn whatever YOU desire.

  ○ The more time and effort YOU put into anything YOU do—especially learning and education—the more successes YOU will enjoy.

- No matter how much YOU want success for your children, they have to want success for themselves, too.

Never embarrass your child, especially not in public

- Praise in public; when necessary, chastise in private.

- Respectfully correct your child.

- Never demean or embarrass your child, especially not in front of others.

- Keep your emotions under control and behave maturely, especially when your child is not.

  - YOU can be stern, impacting, and tough without yelling, hitting, or losing your composure.

Provide your child with the fundamental learning tools

- Make sure your child has:
  - ○ Pencils/pens
  - ○ Highlighters
  - ○ Ruler
  - ○ Paper
  - ○ Loose-leaf or spiral notebooks with pockets
  - ○ Dictionary
  - ○ *How to Be a Great Student*
  - ○ Eraser
  - ○ Calculator
  - ○ Library card
  - ○ Backpack
- If YOU have the resources, also provide:
  - ○ Computer, printer, paper, and CD-R disks
  - ○ MP-3 player

Enroll your child in the best achievement and standardized preparatory test courses that YOU can afford

- Comprehensive preparation is critical to perform well on achievement and standardized tests.

- Prep courses:
  - ○ Decrease fears of the test.
  - ○ Provide important tips and suggestions regarding how to take the test.
  - ○ Provide ample opportunity to practice and simulate the real exam.
  - ○ Provide clues and tips on how to answer questions.
  - ○ Improve your child's performance.

PARTICIPATE!

- Be involved and engaged in your child's education.

- Volunteer to help your child study by reading vocabulary words or asking practice questions.

- Attend your child's events—consistently.

- Turn off your cell phone and pay attention to your child.

- Focus on your child's event, not talking to others.

- Be there and be fully present.

- Ask your child's opinions and thoughts about the event afterwards.

- Positively affirm your child for his/her participation, even if he/she did not play or performed poorly.

- Show your child that YOU are proud of him/her.

Inspect what YOU expect

People do not necessarily do what YOU expect; they do what YOU inspect. Children are no different..

- Review progress reports and report cards carefully.

- Keep an eye out for your child's homework, test, and assignment dates.

  ○ Ask to see the graded assignments when they are returned.

  ○ Discuss the results calmly and lovingly.

- Regularly ask your child: "What did YOU learn at school today?"

  ○ Listen to the response.

  ○ Show genuine interest in the response.

  ○ Discuss the response.

Parent Point #44

Nurture your child

- Love, encourage, support, and positively affirm your child.

- Treat your child with dignity and respect.

- Have time, energy, and attention for your child.

- Participate in your child's life with a smile.

- Do things that your child loves, regularly, even if they are not your activities of choice.

- Listen to your child when he/she is talking to YOU. Maintain eye contact and give him/her your full attention.

- Respect your child's feelings and emotions even when YOU do not understand or share them.

- Smile at and hug your child daily.

  - That gives your child comfort, confidence, and security.

  - That says "I love YOU and YOU are important to me" more than words ever could.

Parent Point #45

*Teach, assist, and help, but
DO NOT COMPLETE
your child's work*

- Do not create bad habits or expectations that "my parent or caregiver will do my work for me."

- Remember that it is your child's work, not yours.

  ○ Therefore, it is your child's responsibility to complete it.

  ○ If YOU do your child's work for him/her, how will he/she ever learn to be able to do it himself/herself?

- Be there to encourage and support your child, but allow your child to complete the assignment.

Make sure your child eats breakfast before he/she leaves for school, especially on test days

Provide your child with a healthy and nutritious breakfast every day, but especially on school days and test days.

- Encourage and provide healthy food choices and eating habits.

- Plan ahead in order to fit breakfast in.

- Make sure that your child eats breakfast every day, no exceptions.

Reward the behaviors that YOU desire

- One of the best ways to get the behaviors that YOU want is to reward or acknowledge your child when he/she does them.

- Most children want to please their parents and receive their parents' approval.

- Children learn what good and bad are from your reactions to them.

- Positive responses are very powerful.

- Positive reinforcement tends to be a better motivator and a more effective tool than negative reactions or punishments.

Teach your child how to prepare

Quality preparation is vital to your child's success in learning.

- Learn then teach the basics provided in *How to Be a Great Student* with your child.

- Review the various lessons on preparation together.

- Help your child practice the various preparation techniques provided.

Quality preparation:

- Builds confidence.

- Allows your child to learn.

- Provides an opportunity to practice.

- Improves your child's ability to think and perform well.

---

*Expose your child
to the world*

Expose your child to the world

- Expand your child's perspectives of what life can be and all that the world has to offer.

- Expand your child's horizons by exposing your child to:
  - ○ Libraries
  - ○ Museums
  - ○ Books
  - ○ Sports
  - ○ Music

- Visit family members who live in different areas.

- Visit friends who live in different places.

- Travel to new places.

- Read together regularly.

- Encourage your child to read the newspaper every day.

Parent Point #50

Travel with your child

Travel is one of the best ways to educate, inspire, motivate, and empower your child to dream.

YOU don't have to do anything fancy. Simple family field trips have a positive impact.

- Expand your child's perspectives and horizons by exploring new places in your area, community, city, or state.

- If YOU have the means, take your child to other states and countries.

- Introduce your child to the world.

- When possible, take your child to see different parts of the land (beaches, mountains, cities, or the country).

- Explore these great ways to "travel from home":
  - Books and magazines
  - Internet
  - Movies and documentaries
  - Family photo albums

Help your child develop an adventurous spirit

- Remove "can't" from your child's vocabulary.
- Support and encourage fresh ideas and creative thinking.
- Encourage your child to be active.
- Provide creative opportunities to learn.
- Limit TV, video game, and computer time to an appropriate amount.
- Do things outdoors with your child.
- Help your child conquer his/her fears.
- Encourage your child to try new things.
- Remind your child that YOU will be there if he/she happens to fall.

Use your summer wisely

- Seek fun ways to expose your child to new things.

- Take a family trip (see Parent Point #50).

- Look to enroll your child in at least one summer camp.

- Summer camps are great tools because they:

  ○ Expose your child to new things.

  ○ Provide your child with an opportunity to meet new people.

  ○ Give your child an opportunity to learn, attempt, and develop new skills.

  ○ Give your child a chance to have fun.

  ○ Provide structure and routine.

  ○ Occupy your child with positive and constructive activities.

CHAPTER SIX

Encourage Your Child to . . .

Parent Point #53

Encourage your child to . . .
"Explore what YOU love"

Why?

- When your child does what he/she loves, it rarely feels like work.

- Your child will put forth a smarter and better effort.

- Chances are the more your child loves something, the better your child will perform at it.

- Your child will be less easily deterred and more committed to attaining his/her own goals.

- It will be easier to get your child to practice and work to get better at what he/she loves.

- It is a fun and connecting way to build and develop new skills.

- Your encouragement, support, and sincere interest in what your child loves validates your child. He/she feels more secure since YOU are participating in something that YOU both recognize is important to him/her.

Encourage your child to . . . "Be patient with yourself"

Remind your child:

- YOU are going to make mistakes, and that is a good thing!

- Do your best every day in class, on your homework, and on all essays and exams.

- YOU will fail at times when YOU attempt to learn.

  ○ Mistakes are a part of learning, so control your emotions when YOU fail.

  ○ Do not get angry.

- A mistake does not imply that YOU are dumb.

- A mistake simply means that YOU have more work to do.

Parent Point #55

*Encourage your child to . . .
"Get to know yourself"*

Ask your child to think about the following:

- What do YOU like?
- What are YOU good at?
- What is hard for YOU?
- What is easy for YOU?
- What would YOU like to be?
- What do YOU love to do?
- What would YOU like to try?
- Where would YOU like to go?

Encourage your child to . . .
"Develop a love and passion
for learning"

- Remind your child that learning new things is fun, builds confidence, and enables YOU to learn more. Tell your child:

  ○ Do not look at learning as a negative experience.

  ○ Approach learning with an open mind and an open heart.

  ○ Try and learn new things every day.

- Recognize and acknowledge when your child attempts or learns something new.

*Encourage your child to . . .
"Always do the best
that YOU can"*

- Offer these tips to your child:

  ○ The best measuring stick is your best, not someone else's.

  ○ Give your all each and every time, and YOU will absorb, retain, and learn more and more.

  ○ Never cheat because YOU are only cheating yourself and misrepresenting who YOU are.

- Encourage your child to always do his/her very best.

- Know what his/her best effort truly is.

- Consistently acknowledge and support your child's best effort.

Encourage your child to . . .
"Respect yourself first"

Remind your child:

- To believe in your right to learn.
- That YOU deserve help.
- That YOU can learn.
- That YOU are not dumb.
- To invest in yourself.
- To protect and honor your education.
- To remain in control of your actions.
- To take pride in everything that has your name on it or that YOU are associated with.

Parent Point #59

→

Encourage your child to . . .
"Communicate with your
educators!"

Remind your child to:

- Ask questions.

- Ask for help.

- Never be afraid to ask for help, clarification, or personal time.

- Talk, write, or e-mail your educators.

- Let people know how YOU are doing, when YOU need help, and how the help YOU received has impacted YOU.

---

*Encourage your child to . . .
"Try new things"*

When your child asks "Why?", tell him/her that trying new things:

- Expands your perspectives on what is possible.

- Allows YOU to discover new interests.

- Helps YOU develop new skills.

- Shows YOU that the sky does not fall when YOU make a mistake.

Encourage your child to . . .
"Own your education"

Remind your child that "getting the most out of your education is up to YOU," so:

- Give it your best effort.

- Ask for help.

- Commit to learn as best and as much as YOU can.

- Turn in work that illustrates your self-respect.

- Make sure your schoolwork is:
  - Clean
  - Neat
  - Not crumpled or wrinkled

- Assume full responsibility of your education.
  - Know exactly what is required to graduate.
  - Learn, know, then verify exactly where YOU stand in relation to the graduation criteria.
  - Correct any errors in your records immediately.

Encourage your child to . . .
"Take pride in everything
that has your name on it"

- Remind your child, that his/her name represents your child, especially when your child is not in the room.

- Self-respect begins with ensuring that everything that has your name on it meets your personal quality standards.

Encourage your child to . . .
"Be tough and strong"

Tell your child:

- Have conviction.
- Have self-respect.
- Fight peer pressure.
- Do not let others define who YOU are or what YOU can be.
- Be true to who YOU are and what YOU believe.
- Find the courage to be who YOU are, regardless of how others treat YOU.
- Define the terms and priorities of your life:
  - Be a leader, not a follower.
  - Stay true to yourself.
  - Do what YOU know and believe to be the right thing to do.
  - Be aware that doing the right thing is not always the most popular thing, and that is okay.

Encourage your child to . . . "Stand on your own"

Remind your child:

- Do your work yourself.

- Respect the school, classroom, and teachers.

- Be responsible and accountable for all that YOU do.

- Never cheat. Do the work yourself, and do your best.

- Honor and respect yourself by staying true to your own principles and values.

- Conduct yourself in ways that honor and reflect who YOU are, not what others expect YOU to be.

Encourage your child to . . .
"Be persistent"

Tell your child:

- Never quit, because YOU are only quitting on yourself.

- Ask for help, every time YOU need it, even if it feels like your educators do not want to give it to YOU.

- Believe and remember: YOU deserve the help and extra time, especially when YOU put in your best efforts daily.

- Keep working on a topic or subject until YOU understand it.

  ○ And yes, sometimes, YOU have to try several times before YOU truly learn something.

- Be patient with yourself.

  ○ Everything worth learning, having, and accomplishing requires commitment, diligent effort, and hard work.

Encourage your child— period

- Know your child's dreams and support them.

- Positively interact with your child.

- Dream with your child.

- Validate your child through loving him/her UNCONDITIONALLY.

- Smile at and hug your child often.

- Believe in your child and remind him/her that YOU do.

- Be an active and positive participant in your child's life.

  - Nothings says, "I care about YOU" more than being physically there.

- Establish and maintain a schedule or routine at home.

- Provide the structure and consistency that your child needs.

CHAPTER SEVEN

LOVE, LOVE, and More LOVE!

Love your child UNCONDITIONALLY— good or bad grades, effort, behavior, or performance

YOU can *not* approve of your child's actions and still love and support your child unconditionally.

- Teach your child through the consistency of your words and deeds that YOU will always love him/her regardless of his/her actions.

- Remind your child that YOU believe in him/her.

- Smile at and hug your child every day—no exceptions.

- Handle mistakes or disappointments calmly and respectfully while correcting the actions and poor choices—not the child.

- When your child makes a mistake:

  ○ Focus your attention and commentary on the actions taken, not the child.

  ○ Be clear about what the proper choices were.

  ○ Remind your child what your expectations of him/her are.

  ○ Finish the conversation with a supportive and loving gesture.

Parent Point #68

*Validate your children—
let them know that YOU love
them just as they are*

- Your child wants your approval more than anything else.
  - Always make sure that your child knows that YOU approve of him/her.
  - Disapprove of actions and behaviors, never the child.
  - Always give your child the feeling that he/she is "good enough" and deserving of the very best that life has to offer.
- Great ways to validate your child:
  - Smile when YOU see your child.
  - Give your child several loving and warm embraces daily.
  - Tell your child that YOU love him/her regularly.
  - Do things that your child loves to do, periodically.
  - "Lighten up!" Relax your pressure and enjoy your child.

Be patient and understanding with your child

- Everyone has bad days or falls short of the target at times, even YOU!

  ○ Be reasonable and realistic with your child's effort, performance, and behaviors.

  ○ Learn to accept your child's best effort.

  ○ Focus on behaviors and choices and the good results will come.

- Love and understanding are incredible motivators.

- Loyalty is earned in times of crisis or failure. Therefore, positively affirm and support your child, especially in pivotal situations.

- Being supportive and understanding does not equal condoning poor choices, laziness, or bad attitudes.

Remind your child that grades are NOT everything

- Grades are very important, but quality preparation, diligent effort, LEARNING, and enjoying the process matter most.

- Learning and developing great study, preparation, and work habits are critical to your child's lifelong success. Focus your child's attention on a commitment to:

  ○ Thorough preparation

  ○ Diligent effort

  ○ Positive attitudes toward learning

  ○ Doing his/her very best

  ○ Learning all he/she can

- The ultimate goals are learning and:

  ○ Being able to recall and retain what YOU learned when YOU need it.

  ○ Applying what YOU learned properly.

  ○ Using what YOU learned to improve and enhance your life.

Support your child's dreams; never destroy them

Support your child's dreams; never destroy them

- Give your child hope; never destroy it.

- Help your child discover and own his/her own dreams.

- Encourage and support your child's dreams.

- Help your child uncover what steps are required to achieve his/her dream.

- Get involved.

- Positively affirm your child by saying: "YOU can do anything YOU set your mind to."

  ○ Those simple words will propel your child further than YOU could ever appreciate.

Teach your child that success is up to him/her

- Tell your child:
  - ○ Your ultimate success is up to YOU.
  - ○ YOU have to make the effort, commitment, and sacrifices.
  - ○ YOU CAN LEARN anything that YOU set your mind to with the proper training, tools, time, and effort.
- Teach your child the four components of learning:
  - ○ Training
  - ○ Tools
  - ○ Time
  - ○ Effort
- Remind your child: "YOU provide the two most important components—time and effort."
- Encourage your child to develop the skills, knowledge, and ability to think, act, and take care of himself/herself.

Parent Point #73

Put your personal educational fears, failures, pains, and defeats aside

- Do not project your negativity toward education onto your child.

- Allow your child to have his/her own educational experience.

- Push your child to pursue his/her dreams, not anyone else's—not even yours.

- Separate any negative experiences, failures, or disappointments in your own educational experiences from your child's educational experience.

Stand on your own principles and share them with your child

- Let your child know your:
  - Values
  - Principles
  - Priorities
  - Passions
  - Interests
  - Personal story/history
  - Expectations
- Children take pride in knowing where they came from.
  - There is no better place to find out about their family history than from YOU.
- One of the best ways to help your child develop his/her own values is through learning about your values and then asking: "What is deeply important to YOU?"

HOW TO RAISE A GREAT STUDENT   161

LIGHTEN UP!

- Take the pressure off of yourself, your family, your child, and your child's educators.

- Have fun with your child.

- Enjoy the process.

- Be a full participant in your child's life.

  ○ Do not miss the experience.

- Give your children room to grow, by not doing "everything" for them.

- Remember that too much pressure breaks things, not strengthens them.

- Develop a good sense of humor:

  ○ It will get YOU and your family though bad times.

  ○ It will help YOU to create and share good times with your family as well.

Love, laugh, live, and learn

Life is an adventure. We all accomplish more with an open mind, a clean heart, love, and a desire to learn new things.

- Do not take things too seriously.

- Teach your child the magical and therapeutic powers of humor, laughter, and looking at the sunny side of life.

- Be the role model and example of what YOU expect from your child.

Parent Point #77

Develop a new family mantra about work, play, and togetherness

- Here's your new family mantra:
  - ○ Work hard.
  - ○ Play hard.
  - ○ Always stick together.
- Family should be the most loving, loyal, and supportive system your child will ever know.
  - ○ Give your best.
  - ○ Have fun as a family, too.
  - ○ Always support one another.

ABOUT THE AUTHOR

Thomas Roberts epitomizes the term "people person." He has extensive experience building, leading, managing, and participating on teams in sports, community, education, and Wall Street. He loves inspiring and helping others become all that they can be.

Roberts has coached, trained, recruited, managed, taught, hired, and developed students, athletes, Wall Street professionals, and our nation's wealthiest families. He has melded the lessons, experiences, and observations from these interactions into a dynamic curriculum for all to use. His curriculum is positive, inspiring, impacting, yet simple to implement.

The content and curriculum are purely action and behavior based. They focus solely on the actions, habits, and choices that students can make that will help them to quickly become better students. His goal is to provide educational training, tips, and tools to help every individual to empower himself/herself through education.

Roberts has been a great student since his formative years at Greensboro Day School in Greensboro, North Carolina. In fact, he received the school's most prestigious award, the Founder's Award, for the graduating senior who best exemplified the school's motto: "Friendship, Scholarship, Sportsmanship."

Roberts went on to receive his BA from the College of William and Mary after successfully completing a double major in economics and anthropology in 1993. Upon graduation, he pursued a longtime dream of professional athletics by playing basketball professionally overseas in Gmunden, Austria, and Dubai, United Arab Emirates. In 2004, he received the Colonial Athletic Association's Men's Basketball Legend Award for his outstanding achievements on the floor in college and off the floor in the business world.

After retiring from basketball, Roberts began a banking career at Wachovia Bank in North Carolina. He left Wachovia to enroll in the MBA program at the Kenan-Flagler Business School at the University of North Carolina at Chapel Hill.

After graduating from the UNC Business School in 2001, Roberts moved to New York to join the J.P. Morgan Private Bank. In 2004, he left JPM to join the Citigroup Private Bank as a vice president in the firm's High Net Worth Group in Washington, DC.

Roberts retired from banking in 2006 to formally pursue his lifelong purpose and passion of inspiring, motivating, and educating others. Since retiring, he has authored two books, built three companies, and spoken to hundreds of students about the power, purpose, and possibilities that education provides. He is the founder and chief executive officer of Roberts Education Corp and the Great Student Network, a positive, collaborative, and educational support network based on Roberts' fundamental belief: "Every Student Deserves a Chance to Be Great."

Despite being the first male on either side of his family to graduate from college, Roberts has achieved tremendous success across athletics, academics, and corporate America. How did he accomplish so many things? The old fashion way—through hard work, a positive attitude, a commitment to excellence, and a relentless pursuit of education.

According to Roberts, "The only way to transcend one's current circumstances and/or to ensure that YOU maintain control over your future is through education."

Empower YOUniversity

MESSAGE AND MISSION

Empower YOUniversity is a multimedia publishing house focused on providing the educational tools and training to empower, motivate, inspire, and train YOU. Our mission is to help YOU transform your life through action-based products that are easy to use, understand, and implement in your daily life.

We recognize that YOU like to access your content in various ways, styles, and formats. Therefore, we produce our content in a variety of media formats so that YOU can choose how, and when, YOU utilize our products. Our content is not only available in traditional print format, but it will also be available in audio book, e-book, podcast, downloadable sections, CD-ROM, and DVD.

For more information, visit our website:

www.empoweryouniversitymedia.com

*"Providing YOU the Fundamentals
to Win in the Game of Life"*

HOW TO BE A
GREAT
STUDENT

The Ultimate Guide
for **YOU** to Learn, Prepare,
and Become the Best
Student **YOU** Can Be

T H O M A S   R O B E R T S

HOW TO BE A GREAT STUDENT

How to Be a Great Student is not just a book. It is a student's:

- A constant, positive, and helpful educational companion for life.

- Detailed road map for success in school.

- Comprehensive educational resource and training guide.

- Tailored support system.

- Personal tutor.

- Inspirational and motivational tool.

How to Be a Great Student is an action-based text that is designed to help YOU become a better student through a clear, simple, and easy-to-understand format, use of language, and structure. Each lesson is presented on its own page and then immediately explained and reinforced on the adjacent page in order to help YOU see the message, grasp and understand it quickly, and then explain "how to use" what YOU just learned and "why" that lesson is important for YOU to know and understand. The chapters are structured specifically to help YOU improve and maximize every aspect of your educational performance and experience.

GREAT STUDENT NETWORK

"Every Student Deserves a Chance to Be Great"

GreatStudentNetwork.com

GREAT STUDENT NETWORK

The Great Student Network is a positive collaborative member community dedicated to one fundamental belief: "Every Student Deserves a Chance to Be Great." The gateway to the network is:

GreatStudentNetwork.com

The website features educating, empowering, and inspiring information for concerned citizens, especially for students, parents, caregivers, educators, nonprofits, and socially responsible companies.

GreatStudentNetwork.com features:

- Great Student Network Awards
  - Student, Educator, and Parent/Caregiver
- Great Student Profiles
- Great Student Interviews
  - Eight Great Student Questions
- Sample Great Student Multimedia Content
  - How to Be a Great Student
  - How to Raise a Great Student
- Great Student Newsletter
- Educational Articles, Lessons, and Tips
- Sponsor Links

NOTES

NOTES

NOTES

NOTES

NOTES